ULTIMATE
CHRISTMAS
TRIMMINGS

C.R.Gibson®
FINE GIFTS SINCE 1870

WREATHS, GARLANDS, & FLOWERS

*Glossy evergreen leaves and colorful
berries have always symbolized the hope
of new life in the depths of a northern winter.
Use them in combination with fresh or dried
flowers, fruit, and nuts to make seasonal
wreaths, garlands, and door swags that
will transform your home into the
essence of Christmas hospitality.*

CHRISTMAS WREATHS

NEUTRAL MUTED COLORS highlighted with shimmery hints of gold and bronze make a perfect palette for inspiringly different Christmas wreaths. Focus on texture, contrasting the natural roughness of reindeer moss, bark, and barley with smooth satin and soft wispy ribbons tied in luxurious bows. Then crown the festive look with a bunch of sparkly berries.

Fresh berries still look good when dried

RUSTIC BARK
Wrap a ribbon around a store-bought bark wreath and tie a bow at the top. Glue a bunch of dried yellow rosebuds under the bow and tie gold-painted wooden hearts to the ribbon.

Gold mesh ribbon

DRIED BERRIES
Wire clusters of fresh pyracantha berries to a strong wire frame and tie a gauzy ribbon in a bow at the top. Leave the berries to dry.

R emember that your design should always and primarily take safety into consideration.

PALE AND INTERESTING
Decorate a store-bought reindeer moss wreath with a bunch of gold artificial berries and two voile ribbons in harmonious colors.

COUNTRY STYLE
Glue a bunch of pyracantha berries
and a wired rosette of ribbon to a
small twisted barley wreath.

BRONZED IVY
Wrap long strands of ivy around a
square piece of wire and spray with
copper paint. Glue on a bronze satin
ribbon tied in a flat bow.

CHILI RING
Thread dried chilies onto a wire
and bend into shape. Glue
together rosettes of wire-edged
ribbon and raffia and wire
them in position at the top.

Dried chilies packed
onto an oval of wire

NUTS AND SEEDS
Glue whole nuts, seedpods, seeds, and
spices randomly onto a store-bought
wreath base and highlight some of them
with gilt creme. Finish with a wire-edged
taffeta bow positioned on one side.

Bundle of
cinnamon
sticks

FESTIVE GREEN WREATH

AN EXTRAVAGANT WREATH on the front door gives guests a hint of the seasonal festivities to be enjoyed inside the house, and this unusual wreath is large enough to adorn any outside door. Be a little different with a homemade diamond-shaped base, and use an eye-catching mix of fresh and dried leaves, flowers, and fruit, brightened for Christmas with shiny baubles in shades of blue and green. To finish, draw the eye to the center with two lavish bauble-trimmed bows made from thick green ribbons edged in gold.

FESTIVE GREEN WREATH Ingredients

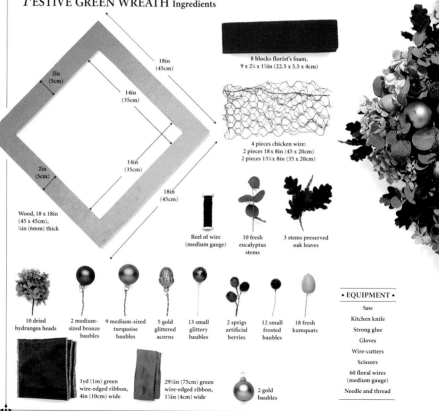

18in
(45cm)

2in
(5cm)

14in
(35cm)

2in
(5cm)

14in
(35cm)

18in
(45cm)

Wood, 18 x 18in
(45 x 45cm),
¼in (6mm) thick

8 blocks florist's foam,
9 x 2¼ x 1⅝in (22.5 x 5.5 x 4cm)

4 pieces chicken wire:
2 pieces 18 x 8in (45 x 20cm)
2 pieces 13⅞ x 8in (35 x 20cm)

Reel of wire
(medium gauge)

10 fresh
eucalyptus
stems

3 stems preserved
oak leaves

10 dried
hydrangea heads

2 medium-
sized bronze
baubles

9 medium-sized
turquoise
baubles

5 gold
glittered
acorns

13 small
glittery
baubles

2 sprigs
artificial
berries

12 small
frosted
baubles

18 fresh
kumquats

1yd (1m) green
wire-edged ribbon,
4in (10cm) wide

29½in (75cm) green
wire-edged ribbon,
1½in (4cm) wide

2 gold
baubles

♦ EQUIPMENT ♦

Saw

Kitchen knife

Strong glue

Gloves

Wire-cutters

Scissors

60 floral wires
(medium gauge)

Needle and thread

Fresh kumquats
add color

Small pieces
of hydrangea
fill in gaps

*H*ere we come a-caroling
    Among the leaves so green;
Here we come a-wand'ring,
    So fair to be seen,
Love and joy come to you,
And to you glad Christmas too;
And God bless you and
    send you a happy New Year,
And God send you a happy New Year.

Old English Wassail Song

MAKING THE WREATH

Before you start, break the hydrangea heads, eucalyptus, and oak leaves into small sprigs, and cut natural stems quite short. Slip pieces of floral wire into kumquats, and twist them through the top of the baubles, so they can be easily secured in the foam.

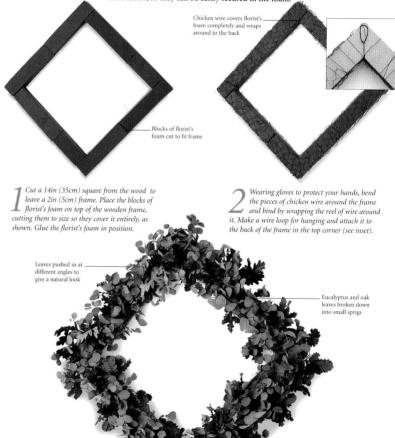

Chicken wire covers florist's foam completely and wraps around to the back

Blocks of florist's foam cut to fit frame

1 *Cut a 14in (35cm) square from the wood to leave a 2in (5cm) frame. Place the blocks of florist's foam on top of the wooden frame, cutting them to size so they cover it entirely, as shown. Glue the florist's foam in position.*

2 *Wearing gloves to protect your hands, bend the pieces of chicken wire around the frame and bind by wrapping the reel of wire around it. Make a wire loop for hanging and attach it to the back of the frame in the top corner (see inset).*

Leaves pushed in at different angles to give a natural look

Eucalyptus and oak leaves broken down into small sprigs

3 *Push sprigs of eucalyptus and oak leaves into the florist's foam, covering both the top and sides of the frame.*

Baubles spaced
fairly evenly to
balance the wreath

4 Fill in gaps with small pieces of dried
hydrangea, pushed in at different
angles to look natural.

5 Push the baubles, acorns, and
artificial berries among the greenery,
using the wire stems to secure them.

Small frosted baubles
look like sugared fruit

6 Fix the kumquats in
place using the floral wire
stems. To finish, glue a small
cheat's bow in the center of a larger
one and wire both to the top of the
wreath. Sew a bauble onto each tail of
the large bow. Suspend from the wire
loop at the back.

DOOR SWAGS

A DOOR SWAG MAKES a stylish alternative to the traditional Christmas wreath, brightening up the house with festive glamor. For the front door, make a robust evergreen swag that will withstand harsh weather, and use dried flowers, scented spices, and pretty ribbons to make more delicate arrangements for doors inside the home.

BEECH TWIGS
Secure beech twigs in a bundle with wire, then tie the bundle with a red raffia bow. Wire tiny exotic fruits and raffia bows onto the branches and finish with a stuffed tree decoration.

EVERGREEN DROP
Starting at the bottom, wire bunches of blue spruce to a stake so that each layer slightly overlaps the one below. Add red glass grapes at the seams and tie two taffeta cheat's bows at the top.

FLORAL CORNET
Remove the leaves from a bunch of celosia and place it in a cone of chicken wire lined with damp moss. Squeeze it to secure the flowers, then cover by pinning on overlapping celosia leaves. Decorate with a spiral of gold braid and hang from a loop of ribbon.

Celosia leaves pinned in place with fine wire

Top edge of leaves folded neatly over

DRIED SWAG
Adorn the front of a store-bought twig-and-spruce swag with cinnamon sticks, dried hydrangea, an artichoke sprayed gold, and artificial apples. Wire or glue the items in place and finish with a glossy double bow.

HOLLY AND IVY BUNCH
Make a flat bundle of blue spruce, holly, and ivy and wire it at the top, tying the bundle with a green taffeta ribbon. Decorate with cranberries threaded onto rings of floral wire.

Miniature wreath made of cranberries

> *T*he holly and the ivy,
>   When they are both full grown,
> Of all the trees that are in the wood,
>   The holly bears the crown.
>
>   English Carol

GARLANDS

BRING THE DELIGHTS of the garden indoors for festive celebrations by making a bountiful Christmas garland for the house. Create a garland with drop swags to fit around a doorway or window arch, lay a long garland down the center of the dining table, or entwine it around stair banisters for sheer flamboyance.

Sparkling artificial berries wired to the center of bows

Double bows in contrasting russet and gold ribbons

GILDED GARLAND
Cover a store-bought drop swag garland of overlapping bay leaves with gilding creme and twist a russet rope around the main section. Decorate the swags with double bows made using contrasting wire-edged ribbons.

Pecans wired to the rope

Store-bought
bark apples

FESTIVE FIR SWAG
*Decorate an artificial fir swag by wiring to
it gold-sprayed dried fruit, nuts, and seeds,
apples made from tree bark, artificial cones,
nuts, and berries. Finish with bows made
from wire-edged ribbon.*

*A*rtificial fir can be substituted
in a garland for those with
allergies.

SPRUCE AND SPICE
*Wire sprigs of blue spruce onto
a thick rope that is easy to drape
around furniture. Cover it with
wired pecans, cones, dried chilies,
and orange slices, and bunches of
twigs and cinnamon sticks.*

FRUIT GARLAND

PACK A LUSCIOUS GARLAND with festive evergreens, fresh red apples, carved dried citrus fruit, dried pomegranates and wired pecans, and add sophistication with shimmering wire-edged ribbons in gold-green and burgundy.

FRUIT GARLAND Ingredients

43in (110cm)

Twig frame

18in (45cm)

Drop swags

Chicken wire, 59 x 8in (150 x 20cm)

Small bag of fresh moss

Reel of fine floral wire

8 bamboo sticks, 10in (25cm)

Fresh red apples add color and shine

*B*erries and apples, holly and vines,
  Make the hearth merry,
    In this season Divine.

Anonymous

**20 sprigs
sarcococca**

**15 sprigs
yew**

**80 sprigs
berried ivy**

**30 strands
ivy**

**15 sprigs
variegated holly**

**45 sprigs
*Senecio greyii***

**21 wired
pecans**

**9 carved, dried
citrus fruits**

**4 dried
pomegranates**

**11 red
apples**

**2½yd (2.5m) gold
wire-edged ribbon
2yd (1.8m) burgundy
wire-edged ribbon**

Dried lime with
carved skin

Long-tailed
double bow
made with
ribbon and
floral wire

Making the Garland

The garland is simple to make using a ready-made twig frame
with detachable drop swags. Buy pecans ready-wired and push
lengths of bamboo stick into dried citrus fruit, pomegranates,
and apples to make stems for securing.

1 *Place handfuls of moss
on the main section of the twig frame,
wrapping the wire around it as you go to
hold it in place. There is no need to cover the
back of the garland.*

2 *Wearing gloves, wrap chicken wire
around the frame, over the moss, and
wind more wire around it to secure.*

Loop attaches swags
to main part and is
used for hanging the
garland when finished

3 *Cover the drop swags
in moss secured with wire
(see step 1). Attach the
swags to the main section using
the loops provided.*

Sprigs pushed in
randomly to give
a natural effect

4 *Push the sprigs of
sarcococca, yew, and
berried ivy into all
sections of the garland, hooking
the stems into the wire.*

5 Push in the strands of ivy, variegated holly, and Senecio greyii *randomly, making sure the chicken wire is completely covered.*

> *Heap on more wood! the wind is chill,*
> *But let it whistle as it will,*
> *We'll keep our Christmas merry still.*
>
> Sir Walter Scott

6 Fill in any gaps on the main section of the garland with the *pecans, dried citrus fruit, and pomegranates, securing with lengths of bamboo stick pushed into the fruit and the frame.*

Dried fruit secured with bamboo stick

Use the loops at the back to hang the garland

7 Push lengths of bamboo stick into the apples and position them along the main section. Finally, make four double *bows in ribbons of contrasting colors. Position two at each end, with a long curl of excess ribbon down each swag.*

FESTIVE FLOWERS

FOR A FRESH TAKE ON Christmas decorations, try an eye-catching arrangement of flowers in traditional festive colors.
Keep each arrangement simple in itself and, for maximum impact, group it with others that are different in height, size, color, and texture. Clever use of plain glass vases in interesting shapes allows the flowers to take center stage.

Classic display of red short-stemmed roses

Dense grouping of ranunculus, gerbera, red anemones, and poinsettia

White anemones cut down short to fit a small square tank

Fleshy stems of red amaryllis stand tall in a vase

Masses of juicy red berries contrast with round red chilies on stems

Brussels sprouts and Romanesco cauliflower florets spiked on bamboo sticks

Squash

Limequat or other exotic fruit

Scented white hyacinth (below) embedded in a tank of damp moss

*T*here is material enough in a single flower for the ornament of a score of cathedrals.

"Paper white" narcissi tied with raffia

Vase lined with sprigs of spruce, then filled with florist's foam

KISSING BOUGH

THE CUSTOMARY EVERGREEN kissing bough is more than just a Christmas decoration: the juicy red apple in the center symbolizes plenty and fertility for the coming season. Hung by the door, the bunch of mistletoe means no visitor can avoid a Christmas kiss! Pack the globe with evergreens, wire brightly colored ribbons into bows, and add gilded fruit, baubles, and tiny Christmas tree decorations for extra-festive sparkle.

Bunch of mistletoe with stems wired and tied with a ribbon

KISSING BOUGH Ingredients

5½yd (5m) steel wire

Carpet tape

Reel of fine floral wire

Apple

1¼in (3cm) bamboo stick

8in (20cm) gold thread

20in (50cm) thick cord

20 strands ivy

Making wired ribbon bows

Zigzag 6in (15cm) of ribbon into three small loops and pinch the ends. Twist a short piece of floral wire around the pinched ends, leaving enough extra to act as a stem. Make 10 of these bows for the kissing bough.

2¼yd (2m) tartan ribbon

50 artificial berries

♦ EQUIPMENT ♦

Wire-cutters

Pliers

Darning needle

Scissors

12 stems mistletoe

Red artificial berries
on wire stems

FORBIDDEN FRUIT
*Make the kissing bough
full to overflowing with lush
greenery, but ensure that
a tempting glimpse of the apple
can be caught between the boughs.*

MAKING THE KISSING BOUGH

The frame is easy to make, using steel wire bought from a roll.
This bends naturally into circles that can be held securely with
strong carpet tape. Variegated ivy leaves lighten the overall color;
choose plain leaves if you require a more dense effect.

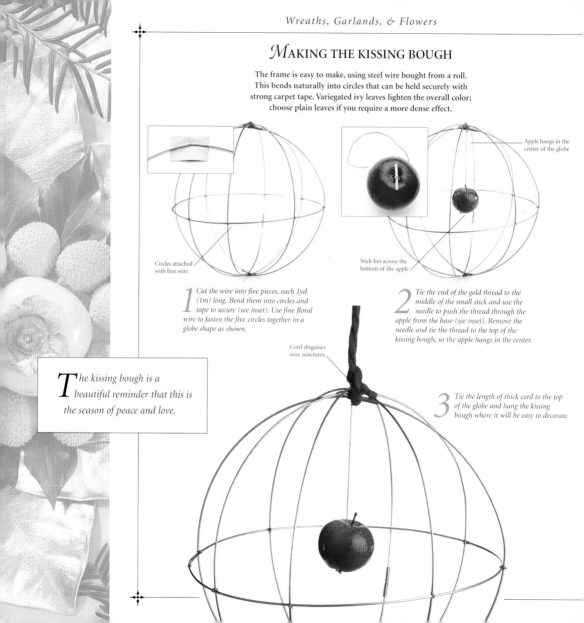

Apple hangs in the
center of the globe

Circles attached
with fine wire

Stick lies across the
bottom of the apple

1 Cut the wire into five pieces, each 1yd
(1m) long. Bend them into circles and
tape to secure (see inset). Use fine floral
wire to fasten the five circles together in a
globe shape as shown.

2 Tie the end of the gold thread to the
middle of the small stick and use the
needle to push the thread through the
apple from the base (see inset). Remove the
needle and tie the thread to the top of the
kissing bough, so the apple hangs in the center.

Cord disguises
wire junctures

*T*he kissing bough is a
beautiful reminder that this is
the season of peace and love.

3 Tie the length of thick cord to the top
of the globe and hang the kissing
bough where it will be easy to decorate.

Weave long strands
of ivy around the
wire circles

Mistletoe suspended
from bottom of globe

4 Wind long strands of ivy around the
wire frame, using floral wire to secure
the pieces as necessary. Keep adding ivy
until the bough is as bushy as required, but
make sure the apple can still be seen.

5 Gather the mistletoe into a bunch,
secure the stems with wire, and tie
with 20in (50cm) ribbon. Use a
long tail of wire to hook the bunch to the
bottom of the ivy-covered globe.

Apple can be
seen through
gaps in the ivy

Artificial berries
add color

6 Wire clusters of artificial berries to the
bough by their stems. Make ten wired
ribbon bows (see page 20) and attach
them to the globe by their wire stems to
finish. Hang in position.

FRUIT AND FLOWER DISPLAY

A MAGNIFICENT TOWER of spectacular fruit and flowers is guaranteed to turn a Christmas banquet into a feast for the eyes. Buy gilded walnuts on wires, twist floral wire through and around stems of roses and hypericum, and push it into litchis and berries in advance to secure them in the display.

MAKING THE DISPLAY

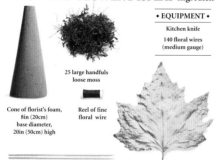

1 Slice off the top 2½in (6cm) of the cone. Fasten the moss to the cone one handful at a time, wrapping the wire around it to secure.

FRUIT AND FLOWER DISPLAY Ingredients

♦ EQUIPMENT ♦

Kitchen knife

140 floral wires (medium gauge)

25 large handfuls loose moss

Cone of florist's foam, 8in (20cm) base diameter, 20in (50cm) high

Reel of fine floral wire

31 bamboo sticks, 10in (25cm) long, broken into 92 lengths

8 plane leaves, sprayed gold

15 red apples

25 persimmons

27 plums

14 small pears

42 roses

30 litchis

14 gilded walnuts

5 apricots

5 passion fruits

8 bunches hypericum

70 ivy leaves

60 cranberries

1 mini pineapple

2 Place the cone on a bed of gold plane leaves. Slipping short lengths of bamboo into the fruit as you work, push rings of skewered apples, persimmons, and plums into the foam. Build up the display by adding rings of small pears, roses, litchis, more persimmons, and plums.

3 Add more rings of gilded walnuts, apricots and passion fruits, litchis, roses, and hypericum. To finish, add cranberries to fill gaps, slide ivy leaves between the layers, and place the pineapple on a bamboo stick at the top.

FESTIVE FRUIT
*Mix brightly colored fruit in
different sizes and textures with
a few gilded nuts and leaves for
special Christmas glitter.*

Pineapple
skewered in place

Hypericum
decorates the top
few layers

Ring of ivy
leaves slipped
between the layers

Cranberries interspersed
among larger fruit

*A fruit and flower display is a
tapestry of nature's bountiful
palette.*

CHRISTMAS LIGHTS & EFFECTS

*Lighting plays an important part in creating
the right atmosphere for a party, be it
old-fashioned candles smelling sweetly of beeswax,
bright modern candles in a bold candelabra, or
the romance of a chandelier made from twigs.
Let quirky lanterns swing enticingly in the porch,
beckoning guests inside where handmade
centerpieces and beautifully decorated mantelpieces
provide a focus for the season's festivities.*

AN ARRAY OF CANDLES

THE SOFT, FLICKERING LIGHT and evocative scent of a host of beautiful candles conjure up the ideal ambiance for a Christmas gathering. Choose from rolled beeswax, twisted, tapered, or square candles, the traditional church variety, molded novelties, or floating flowery candles in festive colors. Reflect the opulence of the season by adorning complementary candleholders with twisted ribbons, cords, and bows.

BEESWAX CANDLES
Choose exquisite beeswax candles for their natural texture and the delicious honey fragrance given off when they burn. Tie thin candles of differing heights together in small bundles to render candlesticks unnecessary.

FLOATING CANDLES
Make beautiful reflections with glittery flower-shaped candles floating in a wide-rimmed, shallow bowl. Scatter petals on the surface of the water for a truly luxurious feel.

Spiral candle decorated with a ring of sparkling glass droplets

Candles tied in bunches should not be lit

String of gold stars wrapped around candleholder

CANDLES IN HOLDERS
Support tall, graceful candles in holders made from glass and gilded wood, here decorated with chandelier-style droplets, twinkly gold stars, and rich satin tassels.

FREESTANDING CANDLES
Jazz up chunky, freestanding candles by adding ribbons and brocade, spiraling cord around them, or tying a gold leaf to the front. Choose novelty candles with unusual shapes and finishes such as glossy or marbled gold.

Blue and gold tassel adorns a church candle

Ribbon and gold-sprayed oak leaves adorn a chunky cream candle

Gold tassel threaded onto sparkly gold elastic wound around a chunky candle

T he warm glow of candlelight is the perfect balm for a case of holiday anxiety.

Decorated Candelabras

TRANSFORM A SIMPLE wrought-iron candelabra into a stunning table centerpiece by winding glossy evergreen leaves around the branched arms and scattering gold foil leaves among rich red roses. Adapt the idea with more dense foliage and artificial grapes, bright satin cord, and colored candles or, for a more formal party, dangle jewel-like beads below navy beeswax candles.

Satin cord hides the black candelabra

LUSH GREENERY
Enliven a candelabra with a bounteous display made by entwining glossy evergreen leaves among the branches. Hang bunches of lustrous artificial grapes from the leaves and add pale green candles to finish.

Christmas tree decoration

Tapered candle made of rolled beeswax

Hanging gold stars catch the light

MEXICAN-STYLE CANDELABRA
Wind brightly colored satin cord tightly around the branches of a black candelabra and add candles in colors to match. Glamorous Christmas tree decorations in matching colors give a festive feel.

EVENING ELEGANCE
Thread delicate blue glass beads and festive gold stars onto fine wire and wrap them in and out of the candelabra branches. Add movement with pretty drops hanging down, and finish with unusual midnight blue candles of rolled beeswax.

FRESH FLOWERS

A fresh arrangement made by winding ivy and roses around a candelabra creates a stunning centerpiece for a special party. If the display needs to last for the whole festive season, use artificial flowers and greenery instead.

Cream candles
complement the
dense colors

Gold foil leaves on
wire stems from cake-
decorating stores

Rich red rose
wired to ivy and
gold foil leaves

Wiring roses

Place an ivy leaf on its stem behind a rosebud so that the two stems lie together. Push floral wire through the bottom of the rosebud and wind it down around both stems to the bottom. Holding the wired stems in one hand and florist's tape in the other, twist the stems to wind the tape around them, binding them together.

*C*hristmas is a time to celebrate
the Light of the world.

TWIG CHANDELIER

GIVE A VINE WREATH A NEW LEASE OF LIFE by turning it into a
spectacular twig chandelier complete with burning candles.
Adorn it with dried fruit, chilies, gilded nuts, and seedpods,
and add sparkling glass droplets to catch the light. Hang
your chandelier over the dinner table for elegant festive
dining or use the glass of a nearby mirror to reflect the
warm glow of the candles around the room.

TWIG CHANDELIER Ingredients

♦ EQUIPMENT ♦
Scissors
Strong glue

Twig wreath, sprayed gold

2yd (1.8m)
gold cord

9 candleholders

Dried
fruit, gilded

6 dried
tangerines,
gilded

1 pine
cone

15 large dried chilies

40 small
dried chilies

6 glass
droplets

6 wired bows
(see page 20)

10 dried tropical
seedpods, gilded

4 pecans,
gilded

9 Christmas
tree candles

Dried tangerine with
gilding creme rubbed
onto the skin

MAKING THE CHANDELIER

1 Cut the cord into three lengths of 24in (60cm). Tie them to the wreath equal distances apart and knot them together at the top. Clip the candleholders around the wreath.

2 Use a strong glue to attach the dried fruit, tangerines, pine cone, chilies, seedpods, and pecans.

3 Hang the chandelier. Position the candles and glass droplets then add the wired bows to finish.

BURNING BRIGHT
Never leave the twig chandelier burning unattended, and make sure you replace the candles as they burn down.

Tree decoration or replacement chandelier droplet from a lighting store

FROSTED CENTERPIECE

DELIGHT YOUR DINNER GUESTS with this abundant table centerpiece, smothered in sparkling sugar-frosted fruit that glitters in the candlelight. Use thick creamy candles, frosted fruit, candied peel, dried flowers, and artificial berries in colors to complement the table setting. If all the fresh fruit is frosted, the centerpiece should last up to one week.

FROSTED CENTERPIECE Ingredients

♦ EQUIPMENT ♦
Knife
Craft knife
Metal ruler
40 floral wires (medium gauge)

Block florist's foam,
9 x 4½ x 3¾in
(22.5 x 11 x 7.5cm)

Silver cake board,
10 x 6½in (25 x 16cm)

2 candles,
6¼in (16cm) high

1 candle,
9½in (24cm) high

15 sprigs
dried leaves

12 dried
hydrangea heads

10 bunches dried,
dyed broom

17 poppy heads

12 bunches
artificial berries

15 dried
pink rosebuds

20 dried
peach rosebuds

10 wired bows
(see page 20)

3 frosted
pears

4 slices candied
citron peel

7 small bunches
frosted grapes

Frosted
purple fig

Candied
green fig

2 candied
tangerines

Candied
greengage plum

6 frosted
kumquats

5 frosted slices
star fruit

A table enhanced by candlelight illuminates the warm glow of those enjoying your holiday meal.

LIVING FLAME
Replace candles before they burn down to the level of the highest piece of fruit.

Candied fruit
does not need
frosting

Bow made with
green ribbon
(see page 20)

Rosebuds wired
into bunches

$\mathcal{M}$AKING THE FROSTED CENTERPIECE

Prepare the frosted fruit in advance to allow it time to dry (see opposite), bend ribbon to make wired bows (see page 20), and twist floral wire around the stems of small bunches of berries, rosebuds, and broom to secure them in the foam.

1 *Measure the diameter of the candles, cut holes for them in the cake board, and place it on the block of florist's foam. Push the tallest candle through the center hole and flank with the two shorter candles.*

2 *Push the sprigs of dried leaves and hydrangea heads into the florist's foam below the cake board.*

3 *Add the wired bunches of broom and the poppy heads between the dried leaves and hydrangeas.*

Push in items at different angles to make the display look more natural

Frosting fruit

1 Wash and dry the fruit to ensure that the skin is clean. Lightly whisk the whites of two eggs in a bowl and use a pastry brush to apply it to the prepared fruit skin.

4 Fill in all the gaps by pushing the wire stems of the artificial berries and rosebuds into the florist's foam.

Individual rosebuds wired into bunches

2 Use a spoon to sprinkle finely granulated sugar gently over the fruit. This gives a more delicate, frosted look than rolling the fruit in sugar.

5 Pile the frosted fruit and candied peel on the cake board to hide it from view completely. To finish, fill any gaps with a scattering of ribbon bows, fastened by pushing the wire stems into the foliage.

3 Leave the fruit to dry on a wire rack. When frosted it will last for up to one week.

LANTERNS

A CLUSTER OF FESTIVE LANTERNS twinkling on the porch guides guests to the front door at Christmas. Buy lanterns ready-made and embellish them with beads, fancy cords, and Christmas tree decorations, or make your own using small glass jars and night-light candles. Use glass paint in rich, jewel colors, add stars and snowflakes with gold paste, or use a sponge-painting technique.

Right, from top to bottom:
MOONLIGHT LANTERN
Spray a metal lantern with gold paint and paint a red moon on one of the glass sides.

RED AND GREEN POT
Paint red and green stripes on a small jar hung from a simple wire harness threaded with beads.

GREEN GARDEN LIGHT
Wrap wire around the rim of a green glass holder, and suspend it from a spiral of wire.

Center, from top to bottom:
TREE LANTERN
Decorate a store-bought lantern with red glass paint and hang it from a length of green cord.

FANCY LANTERN
Embellish a store-bought lantern with gold stars painted on the glass and dangling beneath.

LARGE RED LANTERN
Hang a lustrous moon from the bottom of a red-painted tin lantern suspended from gold cord.

Far right, from top to bottom:
GLOWING GREEN GLASS
Place a small green glass in a store-bought wire holder decorated with luminous beads.

STARLIGHT POT
Paint colored stars, moons, and dots on a red glass pot and hang it from a spiral of green wire.

LARGE OUTDOOR LANTERN
Paint gold stars on the glass of a dark green lantern and add a tall cream candle.

RED CANDLEHOLDER
Hook a loose spiral of wire around a tapered glass holder and glue beads in place on the wire.

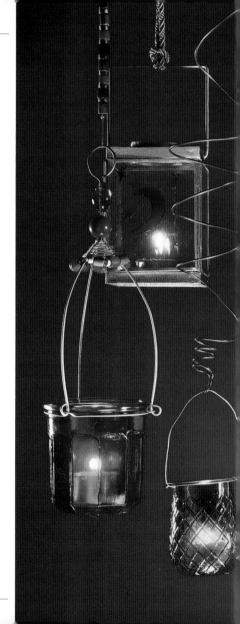

Acknowledgments

C.R.Gibson®
FINE GIFTS SINCE 1870

This book is based on *Ultimate Christmas*, first published in Great Britain in 1996
by Dorling Kindersley Limited, London

Copyright © 2000 Dorling Kindersley Limited, London
Ultimate Christmas text copyright © 1996 Jane Newdick

Developed by Matthew A. Price, Nashville, Tennessee.

Published by C. R. Gibson®
C. R. Gibson® is a registered trademark of Thomas Nelson, Inc.
Norwalk, Connecticut 06856

Printed in China by South China Printing

ISBN 0–7667–6760–4
UPC 082272–46690–6
GB4157

Picture Credits

Photography by Dave King